Asking for Trouble **2**

Take a Hike!

SHERRYL CLARK

Illustrated by Kristin Headlam

Triple3Play

sundance

A Haights Cross Communications Company

Published by
Sundance Publishing
P.O. Box 1326
234 Taylor Street
Littleton, MA 01460

Copyright © text Sherryl Clark 1999
Copyright © illustrations Kristin Headlam 1999

First published 1999 as Supa Dazzlers by
Addison Wesley Longman Australia Pty Limited
95 Coventry Street
South Melbourne 3205 Australia
Exclusive United States Distribution: Sundance Publishing

ISBN 0-7608-4802-5

Contents

First Day, Worst Day

"That's the new kid."

"Yeah, he's from the city."

"Look at his shoes."

Everyone was staring at me, and I hated it. They were just dumb kids in a stupid school. How could you have a school with only fifty-two kids in it? There were more than that in just *one* grade in my old school.

I couldn't see my sister Julie anywhere. She'd run off with her new friend, Lisa. Kenny stood over by the trees with a bunch of other kids. Even though I'd met him over the summer, I wasn't going over to say hi. He'd probably ignore me. No, I was getting out of here. I was going to skip school the first day. All right!

Then the bell rang, and a huge woman in a bright, red track suit strode out of the front entrance. She started yelling, "Inside, you kids. *Now!*"

I couldn't see what her problem was. Everyone except me had already started moving. Her eyes skimmed the playground and landed on me. Her mouth turned down. "You, there!" she shouted. "Report to me. *Now!*"

Great—everyone was looking at me again,

but no one cracked a smile, in case she saw. That was a bad sign. I hauled my backpack along and stood in front of her. My face was about level with her stomach.

"Leo Marrelli?"

"Yeah." Obviously. I was the only new kid in town.

"Yes, Ma'am," she corrected me.

"Yes, Ma'am," I said.

"We use manners at this school, Leo."

There was a pause that she was waiting for me to fill. "Er . . . yes, Ma'am."

"You're in middle school, I see. You'll be in room three—with me. I'm Ms. Crawson."

Right then, I knew it was going to get worse. As I trudged along behind her to the

classroom, I thought about how boring the summer had been, and about how I had decided that, just maybe, school would be better than watching boring TV all day, or riding around on my own. Wrong again. My stomach felt like I'd eaten too many prunes.

Everyone was sitting silently in their seats when we walked in, even Kenny. He waved his hand slightly to say hi when he saw me, but that was it. One seat right in front was empty, and Ms. Crawson pointed to it.

"You can sit there quietly until I've given everyone else their work. Then I'll see what you can do."

I slid into the chair, feeling dozens of eyes poking holes in the back of my head. I got my stuff out while the teacher wrote some things on the board. She talked to a few kids, then she was looming over me again.

"Did you bring your work from your last school?"

"Yes, Ma'am."

"Let's have a look at it."

I handed over my stuff, waiting for the usual comments about my handwriting. Some days, I just couldn't make the pen behave. It scrawled and jumped all over the page. Ms. Crawson didn't say a word, just paged through all of my work and made a funny hissing noise when she got to my math book.

Then she got this giant textbook off the shelf and gave me two pages of exercises to do. They were all hard ones—did she think I was some kind of genius? But everyone seemed to be having trouble, so I just picked up my pen and got started.

I heard whispering and laughing behind me and took a look when Ms. Crawson had her back turned. Two girls stared back and

grinned, then nudged each other and
giggled. Oh boy, that was all I needed.

Chapter 2

Football Failure

At recess, Kenny actually talked to me. Some of the other kids didn't look too happy, especially Ben. I just couldn't figure out why he hated me so much.

"That teacher's pretty weird," I said.

"Ms. Crawson? You've just got to keep on her good side," Kenny said. "She's a good coach."

"Coach of what?"

"Our sports teams. We always win against other schools. Even the little kids here win all the time."

"No bike racing, though," Ben butted in, "so you're out of luck."

"Can I join the team?" I asked.

"You bet," Kenny said. "We're called the Falcons. Ms. Crawson has already begun practice."

At last, something I could actually do. I'd played football with Tony and Tron in the park all the time. Tony's dad put us on his middle school team, and we won second place last year. This year we were going to win. At least, *they* were . . .

I didn't want to think about yet another thing I was missing out on, living in this dump . . . but maybe the football team here would be OK.

"When do you practice?"

"Lunchtime. You gonna play?" Kenny asked.

"Yeah, sure."

Ben rolled his eyes, but before he could
say anything, the bell rang, and it was
back inside for more torture—English.
Ms. Crawson told us to write an essay on
what we did during summer vacation.

How original! What could I write? How I
nearly killed myself on Hollows Bridge? I
scribbled four sentences about riding my
bike and gave up.

At lunch, I couldn't wait to get out on the
field and throw a few passes. Ms. Crawson
appeared with a whistle and a ball under her
arm. A round ball, not an oval one. I
groaned.

"What's the matter?' Kenny asked. "Don't you want to play now?"

"I thought we were playing football."

"Schools here play soccer—less dangerous, less equipment, and more kids get to play."

I shook my head. Stupid school—I should've guessed. I started to walk off, and Ms. Crawson's whistle blasted out.

"Let's go! Marrelli, go to the back of the field for drills until we see what you can do." I trudged away to where she pointed and stood on my own, grinding my teeth. The ball came my way twice. I kicked it back. That was it. The bell rang, and it was time for class again.

Years and years of this stupid place stretched out before me. School, homework, and boring, boring soccer. I couldn't stand it! My blood felt like it was boiling inside me.

No one understood how my whole life was ruined. The things I loved best—hanging around with my friends, riding bikes with them, playing football—were all gone.

And I hated this dump so much, I just wanted to explode into a billion pieces.

Chapter 3

Baiting  the Hook

When Mom got home from driving her taxi, she wanted to know all about school. Julie wouldn't shut up. Her teacher was great. The kids were funny. Lisa had shared her lunch—I wanted to strangle her! I tried to tell Mom how much I hated it.

"The kids are idiots. My teacher is a two-ton monster. And they don't even play football. It's awful, Mom!"

She gave me a funny look and sighed. "It'll get better, Leo. You'll see. Just give it time."

Time! I didn't want time. I wanted to go back to the city.

Every lunchtime we played soccer. Even when Ms. Crawson didn't come out with her whistle, we played. There were six girls on the team, and one was as fast as Kenny. Two brothers, Bos and Ringo, were easily the best. They made the other players look like they were standing still.

Big-mouth Ben never shut up about anyone. At least it wasn't just aimed at me.

"Kick the ball, dope! Pass it, stupid! Speed it up, dummy!" He got dumped a lot. Served him right. The two girls who sat behind me in class sat under the trees and watched. They made me nervous.

All week, I stood near the goal on my own, thinking about being with Tron and Tony and Nick, pretending I was with them and not here. Sometimes it made me feel better—but mostly, I just got angry again, thinking about what I was missing.

Most of the time, the players were at the other end of the field. When the ball finally

came my way, it had big-mouth Ben right behind it. I kicked the ball and dodged him without any trouble.

"You're useless, Slicker," Ben sneered. "Go play basketball with the girls."

I turned, my fist ready, but he was already running back to the game.

"Just wait," I muttered.

On the weekend, Kenny asked me if I wanted to go fishing. I was desperate, so I said yes. It wasn't as boring as I thought it would be. He showed me how to cast for trout, flicking the line and lure out across the water.

He asked me lots of questions about the city.

"What did you do for fun? Just hang around?"

"Are you kidding? This place is dead compared to there. We had lots to do— riding, movies, video arcades, playing football in the park . . ."

He shrugged. "Here we go camping or out to the farms, or fishing or riding—all sorts of things. And I play soccer in the school league."

"My football team's going to win the cup this year," I sighed.

"Without you?"

"That's true. Maybe they won't, without me there." Kenny grinned, and I punched his arm. "Yeah, right."

Chapter 4

Win or Lose

School on Monday was the same. Ms. Crawson seemed determined to make me into a math wizard. I wanted to tell her it was impossible, but I knew she wouldn't listen.

At lunch, she moved me to offense. Ben glared at me from across the field.

Kenny kicked off, and I jogged around, my arms feeling like logs of wood. I couldn't get used to not catching the ball. Someone kicked, and the ball rose into the air, first spinning and then falling to where Bos and Ringo jostled each other out of the way. At the last minute, Ben charged through and slammed into Bos. He knocked him backward into Ringo, and they both fell over with Ben on top of them. Not fair.

That was it, I'd had enough. Everything I hated right then became big-mouth Ben. I ran over and hauled him off Ringo, then swung my fist. I missed his face and barely connected with the side of his head. He staggered back. Then he saw it was me and leaped forward, his own fists up. I was ready for him.

Suddenly there was a big, red wall between us. A huge hand gripped my collar.

Ms. Crawson shouted, "Cut it out! *Now!*" Two seconds later, I was being dragged off the field toward the principal's office.

"Sit there and *do not move!*" Ms. Crawson dumped me on the wooden seat. I sat alone, while all the little kids giggled and pointed. In a few minutes, Ms. Crawson returned and glared at me.

"You're suspended, Marrelli. This is Monday. Don't come back until Wednesday. I've phoned your mother. Good-bye."

I couldn't even get my backpack. Ms. Crawson watched me plod out the gate toward Mom's taxi. I wanted to say it wasn't my fault. Ben started it, he was asking for it—but I saved my breath. No one ever listened. Mom drove home in silent fury. "Go to your room," she said. "We'll talk when I get home."

Our house was deadly quiet, like it knew I was in trouble again and was just waiting for Mom to start yelling. I could hear some of her favorite lines already. "After all I've done for you, Leo. It's like talking to a brick wall. When are you going to wake up?" And if she started crying again . . . I couldn't handle that.

No, I wasn't going to hang around for the explosion. I was getting out of here. I was going back to where I had friends who knew me, who'd stick up for me. It didn't matter how far it was, I was going back to the city. Then no one in this dump would have to worry about Leo Marrelli anymore.

Chapter 5

The Long Road South

My backpack was still at school, so I had to take Mom's overnight bag. I packed some bread, ham, cheese, a big bag of cookies, water, and four apples. I shouldn't have taken Julie's store of chocolate, but I needed it more than she did. I'd pay her back. It was a promise.

I threw in a change of clothes, my jacket, and my old school cap. Mom could send the rest of my stuff later, when she calmed down.

I checked my watch—11:30. Time to go, before Mom got home from work.

As I rode out of town, I checked around to see if anyone was watching, but the whole town seemed deserted, as usual. In twenty minutes, I was out on the road, heading south.

It felt so great to be free of that dump—the school, Mom, being yelled at. The wind whistled past my face, and my legs powered the pedals like I was in the *Tour de France*.

Between signposts, there were long stretches of empty road. Once in a while, an old farm truck or car passed me, but I kept my head down. In two hours, I had covered about sixteen miles, but there were some big hills coming up.

I stopped by a gate on the side of the road and ate a ham sandwich and an apple. My

water wouldn't last long, but I figured I could refill the bottle in the next town. When I set off again, my legs felt a bit sore, but they soon got going again.

I kept seeing rabbits scooting around, and once I even saw a fox. At one farm, a shaggy, black dog ran out and tried to bite my wheels. "Get away, get off!" I yelled, and finally, he ran back down the driveway.

When I reached the main highway, I knew I was really on my way. The further away from that dump and that dumb school, the better.

This road was busier, with cars and trucks whizzing past every few minutes. I had to stay on the dirt edge, dodging bumps and holes, but I kept pedaling. I'd stop for a rest in another half hour.

I never heard the eighteen-wheeler behind me. I was too busy keeping my bike out of the loose gravel—but I sure heard the truck's horn. It blared so loudly that I jumped in my seat. I fought to keep the bike straight. I entirely forgot about the backdraft huge trucks made.

Whooosh! It was like a tornado picked me up and tossed me sideways. Suddenly, I was heading straight for a huge tree. My handlebars wouldn't turn. At the last minute

I wrenched them to one side, but it was too late. The bike kept going. I hit the tree with a crunching thud, and the world went black . . .

"Oh, thank God, he's not dead!"

The voice sounded familiar, but I didn't want to open my eyes. Everything had gone from black to blinding light.

"Watch his arm, Mrs. Marrelli. It's twisted."

I knew that voice, too, I just couldn't quite . . . "Use your radio to call an ambulance."

"Can't we put him in my car?"

"He's got blood on his head. We learned first aid in school. I don't think we should move him."

"You're sure? OK. I'll call an ambulance."

There was a scuffling noise, and I heard the funny crackling noise that two-way radios make.

Her voice was back. "They're on the way. Are you sure we shouldn't move him? Oh, Leo . . ."

That had to be Mom. No one else said, "Oh, Leo," like she did.

"I'm sure he'll be all right, Mrs. Marrelli." That was Kenny, and he sounded like he didn't believe what he was saying. All I knew was that both my head and my arm were screaming. I never realized pain could be so huge. Everything went dark again.

Chapter 6

Small-Town Telephone

The next time I woke up, it wasn't so bright, and I tried opening my eyes. I blinked a few times and saw a tile ceiling with lots of little holes in it. I tried to move my head, but it had a big gauze turban on it.

"Leo? Are you OK? Can you hear me?"

"Yeah, Mom." She was clutching my hand too hard, but I didn't say anything.

"Thank goodness—I thought I'd lost you. What on earth were you up to?"

Good old Mom. First I was dead, now I was in trouble.

"I was going home, Mom," I whispered.

"Leo, your home's with Julie and me."

I didn't have any argument left in me. My left arm had a cast on it, and I could feel bandages on my leg as well. At least the pain had shriveled to a dull ache.

"Do you hate it here that much?" That was Kenny on the other side of the bed.

"I don't know. It's just . . ." I felt too tired to say any more. Then a question popped into my head. "Mom, how did you know where I was?"

"A couple of people saw you riding out of town. Then Pop Jensen said his dog had run out after some kid on a bike. Oh, and Dottie Smith stopped me and said she'd passed you on her way back from her garden club meeting."

"Great. I thought I was being the invisible man."

"The small town you think is so nosy probably saved your life, young man," Mom said sternly.

"Yes, Mom," I muttered.

"Hey, I've got to tell you," Kenny said. "Ms. Crawson suspended Ben, too."

"Yeah?"

"She seems to think you're pretty good at math," said Mom. "She wants to give you special coaching for some competition— seeing as how you won't be playing soccer for a while."

"Me? Math? Are you kidding?"

"And we thought when your arm is better, you could coach us at football," Kenny added.

Mom squeezed my hand again. "Leo, you can't go back to the city. I'm sorry, honey, but we're here to stay." She sounded sad, but determined.

I wasn't fighting any of that right now . . .
maybe tomorrow. I closed my eyes and
drifted off to sleep.

About the Author

Sherryl Clark

Sherryl Clark has been writing stories, poems, and plays for nearly twenty years. Her first children's book was called *The Too-Tight Tutu*. She teaches writing and editing classes, and also helps people to publish their own books.

Sherryl lives with her husband and her daughter, two cats, and six chickens.

About the Illustrator

Kristin Headlam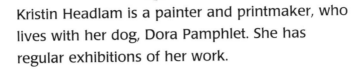

Kristin Headlam is a painter and printmaker, who lives with her dog, Dora Pamphlet. She has regular exhibitions of her work.

To supplement the income of a starving artist, Kristin teaches painting and illustrates books.

Kristin will try anything that comes along, as long as she gets to keep painting.